MW01058269

Faithful

Helen Stetson

WORD & SPIRIT
PUBLISHING

Faithful
Copyright © 2023 by Helen Stetson
ISBN: 978-1-685730-20-8

Published by Word and Spirit Publishing
P.O. Box 701403
Tulsa, Oklahoma 74170
wordandspiritpublishing.com

CONTENTS

1   *Jubilate Deo Omnis Terra* 1

2   Genesis 4

3   We Must See Clearly the Past........................6

4   Melvin's Creek 10

5   A Road Not Taken.. 12

6   Up Ahead.. 15

7   The Watchman 17

8   Lost..19

9   The Christmas Star 21

10 Some People...23

11 Peaceful 26

12 *Amor Patriae*...28

13 Rules to Live By... 30

14 Fort Sumter Sentinel 31

15 The Oysterman...33

16 A Tale of Two Centuries 35

17 Flashbacks...37

18 Drying Out 39

19 Working Girls...41

20 Great Heron Pond 43

21	Gold Rings	45
22	A Place by the River	47
23	The Climate	49
24	A Fifth Season	50
25	What Took So Long?	54
26	Gratitude	56
27	I'm Nobody	58
28	Winter's Coming	60
29	Devotions	62

1

Jubilate Deo Omnis Terra

(O be joyful, all the earth)

I meandered down to the river
as I often do,
and as I slowly ambled,
the river rambled too.

Three white stones
lit a light along the path.
Under a spreading, shedding
oak tree lay a mushroom cap.

A gentle rain was falling,
scrubbing pollen from the air,
a cleansing for the soul,
giving thanks for being there.

Adjacent to the river grew
twenty-two thin trees,
lined along the seawall
leading to a major sea.
The river trees were reverential
as they bowed their heads in prayer,
comforting their fallen limbs,
giving thanks for being there.

A woman at the seawall
before the crossing of a garter
had been given doctor's orders
to gaze upon salt water.
The sea is His, for He made it,
the earth and every race,
dwellers high and lowly
of equal time and space.

A woman heard a calling
as she walked nearer to the water,
her hem reflecting heavenly gold
on God's own living daughter.
A buzzing and a humming
came from an audience of bees,

from four redheaded cardinals
applauding from the trees,
from fireflies blinking
their tiny fairy lights,
a nighthawk's wings dipping
as he took off in flight.

The purity of water is that
on which all life depends,
taking care that every mile
of the river never ends,
as every single creature—
even snails in sandy dirt—
every single species
has potential to be hurt.

True believers don't have time
to wallow in the muck,
to waste their life's potential
protesting in disgust.
Verily it is said to them,
pure and tried and true:
"Trust in God with all your heart,
just as God has trust in you."

Genesis

(Slave House, Gorée Island, Senegal)

This is an origin story.

Over a rolling, pitching sea,
an unsteady vessel approaches
an unforgiving black shore.
Whispered pleas from thirsty lips
     remain unanswered;
soundless screams from tribal eyes
     remain unnoticed.

Buying and eventual selling is the mission;
traders brag and barter amongst themselves
as their precious shackled cargo is
stacked like cordwood in the hold,
trapped like beasts of burden in the guts
of the sinful sailing ship.

An outgoing tide pulls and lifts
the gunmetal Atlantic swells, stretching west
relentlessly, purposefully
toward commercial profits,
docking, at last, at a waterfront landing.

Torture continues on fertile soil:
Strange tongues berate,
broad backs lashed,
orders from the overseers obeyed,
judged with no jury.

marked and measured
mouths of African rivers
spewed forth wave after wave
of heartsick suffering,
as the doors of no return
never reopened.

3

We Must Clearly See the Past

They were renegades, running;
they were heretics, hurting;
they were escapees, espousing.

They were exiles, exploring different options;
their stocks were low, practically penniless;
they had no royal connections, no land grants,
no courtesy titles, no stakeholders,
        no deep pockets.

They were persecuted parishioners who
        traveled abroad,
not to a tax haven, certainly not to heaven
        on earth,
but to a wild land, with their outlandish ideas.

With grit and great determination,
        they conceptualized a nation,
a compact written offshore before any dissension
could break their spirits, their purpose in coming.

With unimaginable sacrifice,
        they erected shelters for protection
from hostile storms, from a frozen wilderness,
        from fierce strangers,
by arriving with no water in wells,
        no welcoming fire to sit for a spell
and spin a yarn about the ship's crossing;
        they were vulnerable
to attacks and to ridicule from people back home,
but they pressed on.

And it is true there were no slaves onboard
        their ship;
they did not drop anchor in the bay to
        exploit labor: they *were* the labor;
they were the field hands; they were the miners;
        they cleaned up

after themselves; they were their own doctors
        and nurses and medical
administrators; they were the hospital,
        the emergency room, the EMTs;
they provided urgent care; they took care
        of their own; they were the case workers,
        answering the late-night distress calls,
        the conscience of their communities.

When they were afraid, they prayed:
they prayed for divine justice, for deliverance
        from oppression;
they prayed for strength for their struggles,
        passionate pleas to be free;
they prayed with energy, haunted by those
        who did not make it safely.

They kept their British birthrights, the customs
        of the country,
creating a new England with exceptions,
such as disavowing the bow,
nor curtsying to any old king or queen
or any old lord or lady; just check today with
        Slim Shady

if people in Detroit rap to "God Save a King"
or if students in Beloit pledge allegiance to
          a queen.

These pilgrims thrived by hard work,
          but were not physically abusive,
only if one considers splitting logs and
          feeding hogs punishment;
there is a difference between suffering
          and survival;
helping themselves and helping each other,
regarding neighbors not as contemptible,
but hospitable.

Unfettering from restraining forces
were choices not taken lightly,
especially when referring to spiritual direction.

We are the beneficiaries of their
          motivated destination
as we inherit and inhabit their courageously
          built colonies,
ever mindful of what we must clearly see—
their legacy.

4

Melvin's Creek

Melvin is a fisherman
as was his daddy
as was his daddy's daddy.

Melvin has a boat
left to him by his daddy,
a flat-bottomed boat,
a jon boat.

Melvin's daddy has gone down
the river of time,
but the jon boat remains—
a rugged boat, a hardworking boat,
like Melvin and his dad and his dad's dad.

Melvin is fishing on the river,
fishing for trout on the river he has known
         all his life,
on the river he calls his own.
He fishes alone with his memories for company,
remembering what his daddy taught him:
that when there is an obstacle,
hop over it.

If you were lucky enough to meet Melvin,
to know him, he would tell you that he has had a
happy life, a peaceful life, but that his greatest joy
is serving the Lord. And this is Melvin's story—
who lives near Melvin's Creek, but it could be any
         Melvin
in any village, in any small town, in any city,
         in any country,
anywhere in the whole wide world.

5

A Road Not Taken

Here is a hard truth:
even though I tell myself I am perfect and
      free from sin,
I have been a sinner again and again.

I have been led into temptation, surrounded by it,
      nearly drowning from it,
wallowing in it, swallowed up in it,
red-hot while pretending I was not.

And then, God extends
an invitation with a knock on the door:
you don't need to hide your corrupt self anymore;
your secrets are known as you weep on the floor,
with excuses so lame, feeling nothing but shame.

At the threshold, my twisted soul is greeted by
a generous ghost, who heals, by grace,
        degenerates like me;
who does not boast that he has lifted up so-and-so
        but asks politely,
"May I come in?" saying, "Be not bereft,
        left to depravity
and sin, you can be changed by the power of
        My holy name."

Imperfections unmasked, it can be a simple ask
to be given a second chance,
        a hope for redemption;
there is always a road to be taken,
        one of bad habits and pain,
but there is also another road in a different lane,
one of forgiveness with renewal to gain.

A divine benefactor does not shield us from sin;
that is our conscience, which comes from within,
from reining it in, from the courage to confess
that our past has been duplicitous, deceptive,
a God-awful mess.

I promise myself to open His gift,
  and this is the gist:
to turn away from the wrong,
  the burn and the blight,
to travel the regulated way to the right.

6

Up Ahead

An afternoon sun flashes
through my windscreen,
alternating blinks, long-leaf pines
leaving dappled shadows
on the long road home,
past a wild turkey run,
not a cloud in a faultless sky,
geese flying in flawless formation,
snowy egrets launching.

The dusty road is filled with tractor trailers,
construction trucks,
pickup trucks hauling gardening cages with
rusty rakes wobbling like last-minute passengers
on a crowded bus.

On the far horizon,
through my mind's eye, is a movie scene
with a young female,
both hands on her bike:
one hand, the hand of reason;
the other, the hand of faith.

In a moment of clarity
when she intermingles this world with the next,
she loses everything except her faith,
which transcends all understanding.

On the near horizon,
wood storks nest in trees,
a black-faced fox squirrel dashes into my lane
acting like a child with no thought of danger,
acorns hidden in both cheeks like a jewel thief
running in circles. I swerve to avoid hitting
        the squirrel,
who is only thinking about tomorrow,
while tomorrow is worrying
about other things.

7

The Watchman

Many of us watch birds;
we are used to standing still,
sometimes for hours on end,
on grassy knolls or hills.

We are quiet; we do not move;
we dare not make a sound;
we respect our fellow birders,
compassionately bound.

Our heads are up, our ears attuned
to hear familiar calls,
or mournful notes like a bugler's "Taps,"
played when a soldier falls.

We are good at watching and waiting
in sunny days or on those with rain;
what we do not do is watch our watch
again and again and again.

8

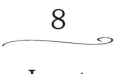

Lost

I was prepared to like you,
to learn from you,
as a learned man,
as a mentor.

I read you,
remembered your name-calling,
your frantic search for synonyms
for other names for which there is
only one name.

Your redundancy was profoundly disturbing,
tomfoolery disguised as profundity,
yet who am I to question arched shape
so carefully crafted?

I am but a sleepy poet,
universally not consulted,
and there you go, unafraid,
using mystical words, wide awake
in the body of your woke work.

I should be insulted—
a slap to my face
for my latent stupidity—
as once again you lost me
with your spiritual pomposity.

I need something more certain,
more truthful, less secular, revelatory
before daybreak.

9

The Christmas Star

Once every eight hundred years,
planets align to produce
a star divine,
a spontaneous sparkle,
a majestic illumination,
prompting attitudes of awe,
like the Magi saw
in the night sky.

While on the ground
in the light of day,
infections are rising,
hospitalizations climbing,
short-term suffering
with multiple deaths
affecting multitudes,
a pandemic so effective

no one is protected;
even the strong and steadfast
couldn't last.

Yet couples on yachts,
sailing aimlessly from sea to sea,
take selfies from deck chairs—
twin flames of self-deceptions,
not noticing thunderheads
gathering over the mountains
never glancing upward
to stargaze without pollution,
aware only of atheistic reflections.

Distance doesn't truly describe
a lifetime of non-compassion,
a legacy of self-protection,
asking God's help
through prayer and supplication
to plan a vacation.

10

Some People

Some people stayed home,
worried about the Wuhan market;
the lab and the bats wondered
what kind of research
while other people went to work:
first responders, cops on the beat,
doctors and nurses and hospital staff,
funeral directors told to expect
two million dead people,
which meant everyone was scared,
and no one was dancing.

Some people shopped for water and food
for their families and neighbors,
stockpiling as if it were the end times,
washing hands, disinfecting groceries
as if their kitchens were fallout shelters.

Some people, such as the homeless,
still camped on the streets, slept on church pews,
as other people lost their homes,
        forced to downsize,
and younger people left their new homes
        for their old homes,
to live with aging people, thankful to have
        a roof once again,
but nobody was dancing.

Some people stayed home,
with death tolls rising,
flights grounded, borders closed;
anxious people met their shadows lumbering
reflected on a door frame, menacing, numbing,
as they shuffled down a hallway,
unable to sleep.

Some people cancelled summer:
trips to the shore, mountains, national parks,
pools, petri dishes for the pandemic,
as other people missed celebrating
the four hundred years
since a sailing ship left
for Plymouth.

Some farmers planted crops in the fall
for themselves and extra for food banks,
as some politicians promised further lockdowns
and an unnaturally painful winter.

Some people Zoomed meetings,
         weddings, funerals.
Some people taught children from home.
Some people arranged a dinner of thanks,
thankful they were still breathing,
waiting for a shot,
not dancing.

Some people in churches lit the first
         Advent candle
with only the rector and the reader attending,
lit the candle symbolizing hope:
hope for a healing for all mankind,
hope for settled minds,
hope for reconciliations,
hope for new dawns of dark clouds lifting,
hope to begin dancing once again.

11

Peaceful

When the curtain falls,
will you hear the Savior's call?
Will you hear a waterfall?
Hear a black crow's *caw-caw*?

Will you hear flapping wings?
Will you hear a choir sing?
Hear a drumming counterpoint beat?
The musical rhythms of marching feet?

Will you hear the raindrops' sound?
An army of bullfrogs down by the pond?
A country band playing guitar riffs?
Mighty waves crashing on Dover's cliffs?

Will you hear a loud baritone?
Or a soloist on a xylophone?
A piano, violin, and cello trio?
An opera tenor's emotive brio?

Or the peaceful quiet of a silence deep,
the peaceful silence of a lasting sleep?

12

Amor Patriae

The country is on fire:
training facilities burned, buildings in ashes,
        old-growth forests leveled,
homes subject to invasions and oftentimes worse,
children displaced and disheveled,
sidewalks as blankets.

Time is not on our side.
Washington, crossing the Delaware,
has abandoned ship, surrendered, lost face,
and now that valor from the first president
        has disappeared,
what has reappeared in its place?

Patriotism expects loyalty
from *We The People*, who are in charge.
Ethical behavior takes many forms,
at the very least discerning the difference
between right and wrong;
not more enamored with an East Asian gong
over our cracked and battle-torn Liberty Bell—
what is going on?

My views, simplistic maybe,
      are perhaps heterodox,
while in my mind they are orthodox:
amor patriae, from Latin to English,
means the same overseas to our friends,
      the British.

Medical directives—*First Do No Harm*—
apply to nations we support and those we arm;
defense from the military equals security
within a legal framework—
not anarchy.

13

Rules to Live By

Use a small *i*
when talking about yourself.

Use a gimlet eye
for signs
for another point of view
for proof of God's wonders.

14

Fort Sumter Sentinel

Viewing the harbor
from the other side,
with a low tide,
I am the sentinel,
covered in nettles,
surrounded by ice plants,
shading my eyes
from a desolate scene—
I am the sentinel.

Metallic sparks
from channel waters
ignite toward cannons;
flat rocks, immovable and rigid,
as they also guard
the ruins of the fort.

Littering the sacred grounds
are oyster shells, crushed, abandoned,
while an ancient wharf is scarcely visible,
washed away by weak foundations.

No trace of a dead soul—
just the sound of lapping water,
the silent flapping of a butterfly,
winging his way farther south.

Here lies a cemetery with no headstones,
no cavalry charged to the rescue,
no more time to honor these men,
for the early birds have risen,
the bloodred sunrise no longer lingers,
the ferry cuts a wide swath,
as laughing gulls dip and frolic at the bow.

15

The Oysterman

With a fiery orange morning sky
and a dead low tide,
the oysterman guides his skiff
aside a riverbed,
among mud mounds and marsh grass
toward hidden treasure.

It is not work for desk-bound folks.
Harvesting oysters means filthy boots and
          dirty gloves,
cold mornings with layers of warm clothes.
Oyster shells are nature's razorblades,
sharp as a knife, quick to the cut.

The oysterman knows the ways of the water
as the farmer knows his fields.
Carefully culling from a base shell,
hammering off mature oysters,

he throws back the smaller clusters
for future growth. Wild oysters need
best practices to replenish.

Wintering shorebirds fly by;
a great blue heron stands upright like a statue;
oyster catchers with bright bills scrounge
for the catch of the day.
The oysterman eyes the free-flowing river,
eyes in harmony with the waterscape.

The tide is rising—
time to return dockside with the cash crop.
Some choose a cubicle indoors for their
          office space:
the oysterman works in natural light.

16

A Tale of Two Centuries

Reading a factual book about political families
in fifteenth-century Italy,
fighting to keep their power,
fighting to gain power,
schemes involving crooked bankers
and rich friends,
changeable, slimy serpents
inciting supporters,
conspiracy stabbings
under the cover of darkness,
casting slippery shadows
over the scales of justice.

At the same time, living in real time
in twenty-first-century America,
experiencing déjà vu plot twists
six hundred years later,
thus questioning
whether our foundations are fragile,
whether the wicked and the violent
are able to pervert law and order—
isn't it the same old, same old,
sad story?

17

Flashbacks

Fading light
from dark to black,
blown tires on the road,
flashbacks.

Go slow
to avoid backflow;
V's in the know,
says too much,
dippin' and dappin',
she's not blabbin',
but it's not her show;
she doesn't wanna carry that load;
that's not her goal.

Late nights
are nothin' but trouble,
dealin' with pain, with broken-down rubble.
Cars jacked up one after the other,
It's not worth the bother—
partyin' 'til dawn,
sneakin' and cheatin',
lyin' and beatin'.
Nobody's home
except the young—
alone.

Go fly a kite
if you wanna get high;
keeps your feet on the ground,
stops the runaround.
It's no skin off my teeth—
you can do the worse.
I'm in bed early
with a Psalms verse.

It's not just the scene that gets wrecked;
it's your self-respect.

18

Drying Out

Three compact-bodied cormorants
arrived at an inland pond
flavored with large-mouthed bass.
Three wet cormorants
perched on a pier
as a freshwater alligator
churned tracks,
chugging along in a straight line
through placid water,
like an old-fashioned steam engine.

Three confident cormorants
opened expansive wings to dry,
flapping in tandem front to back,
sitting comfortably on their platform;
fishing and diving birds doing neither,
stretching out their wet wings—
gangly, guttural birds
handsome in their own skin.

A great egret stood watch high on her nest;
a runaway ring-tailed raccoon snuck around,
as the crafty cormorants caught afternoon rays,
drying out by slants of a softening sun
as if they didn't have a care how long it took
or somewhere else they needed to be,
as if the pier was their locker room,
admiring their mirrored reflections
in the unruffled pond water.

19

Working Girls

Girls at the wheels of pickup trucks,
construction trucks, manning tow trucks,
carrying heavy loads, fording different roads.

Girls are super, working super-important jobs;
girls are superintendents, supervisors,
essential scientists on super colliders.

Girls are first responders: they start the IVs,
type vital stats into computers, alert the ICUs,
meet the ambulances, ensure safety,
        organize mobility—
seven days a week monitoring information
through federal closures, even the one honoring
the birth of our nation.

Girls are doctors in charge of the situation;
girls are technicians taking X-rays, stapling
       the wounds;
girls are an integral part of the team—
sometimes the whole team.

Girls sashay down sidewalks in town,
glossy hair streaming in the wind,
chatting about what could be 'round the corner,
cheeks pearlescent pink from exercising—

Exercising their right to move fast,
flexing their muscles, individually
passionately and philosophically free to be
whatever they want to be.

20

Great Heron Pond

A blue heron delicately tiptoes
over property boundaries with no fear,
moving noiselessly on her high, stilted legs
as if stalking a skittish deer.

Quietly bending her long, thin beak
elegantly down her neck,
pecking at tiny insects there,
eating a midday snack.

After the bend, a quick, precise snap,
peering into the pond like a pro,
like a stealth bomber homing in on a target,
the heron majestically posed.

Her patience will be rewarded;
her menacing bill rules the day,
controls the hunt without much of a battle—
she hungrily sniffs at her prey.

When what to our wondering eyes should appear,
but a bald eagle building a nest—
swoops in and grabs the fish from her mouth.
Heron: good effort. Eagle: the best.

21

Gold Rings

Question for the day:
Does help come
from a man with gold rings
and all the riches in the world
as easily as it comes
from a man with filthy clothes
without a dime to his name?

They say
that clothes make the man,
one with folds of belly,
the other as thin as a walking stick.

It is wishful thinking
to have them trade places,
like trying to catch
lightning in a bottle,

But if we are kept in the dark
about their true selves,
how do they reveal
their inner light to you?

22

A Place by the River

Shirtsleeves and sunshine,
a swoosh on sneakers,
white earbuds and a backpack—
a bike ride down to the water.

Narrow paths mean a nod
to tourists, to townspeople,
to the man with plans
concerning the family park,
as preservationists, understanding
the soothing benefits from the river view.

A father and a mother
lend a protective hand to their child,
trotting on the gravel stones
toward the banks of the river,
toward the dock on the river,
toward the magnetic pull of the
swiftly flowing, wide water.

Under a cerulean sky,
a circle of women near the wooden church
have brought lawn chairs and camaraderie
to their place by the river,
one wearing a dress
the color of hyssop.

23

The Climate

You can control
temperature
inside
hot or cold
on a thermostat.

As far as
temperature
outside
cold or hot
you cannot control that.

Additionally,
who among us controls
God's breath?

24

A Fifth Season

Blood flowed in and out of the lighthouse,
all the way to the White House,
first occupied by Adams,
and now Madison
had moved in.

Outside a cottage door,
people began to ask for more
protection: armed to the
core, the British were
coming, again.

Old versus young were put to the test
(by 1783, young was clearly the best).
But 1814 was about domination
over the U.S. Constitution
and maritime rights.

In Louisiana, the stage was set:
an old major general verses a brash young brevet.
The mightiest navy
the world had ever seen anchored sixty ships
in New Orleans' sights.

Sixteen hundred Brit soldiers embarked as
   fierce fighting men—
no contest at all for Andrew Jackson,
his ramshackle army, underdog in the fight,
established Line Jackson for the Left Bank
   and Right—
and then, lo and behold,
Jackson won.

The battle began on December 14.
If Britain prevailed: a stronghold guaranteed, but
the Treaty of Ghent ended the 1812 War.
They could have saved themselves trouble
   and toil.
Jackson swore not one night on our soil—
not one.

Yet the Brit major general deviously saw
their army was ragtag and had never before
scored a single land victory against the
	British elite—
easy pickings, he just couldn't resist;
he just couldn't miss the opportunity to score.

Now, I don't mean to wax nostalgic
(then give me a better word for it), but
when the British soldiers were done and gone
(it seemed like in a minute thirty),
their battle cry was hollow, hung out to dry,
defeated by Jackson, who barely had to try
or even get his hands dirty,
who had a higher-grade uniform as a brevet,
giving him certain benefits:
a reward for service outstanding,
a thinker and a doer with no grandstanding,
by any standard or measure
a national treasure.

Our task is to consider the good and the bad,
not crucify a man for a job that he had.
On balance preserving a nation
and the battle he won
should have us remember all that was done.
Instead a forgotten victory,
a man from the backwoods of Tennessee
fought for the win, not today's spin.
Why we are not mindful, I don't know the reason,
other than the root cause:
a silly season.

25

What Took So Long?

I wasn't ready.
I wasn't prepared.
I hadn't thought things through.
I hadn't devoted enough time.
I was preoccupied.

I was focused on other things
(hair, makeup, wardrobe).
I was very, very busy
(coffee, lunch, nap, dinner).

I guess I was in massive denial
as I cleaned up messes,
envisioning dangers
from foreign strangers.

Too many balls in the air.
Too engrossed by bats in the belfry.
Too subjected by mold and mildew on weeds.
Too absorbed by biting flies and Daddy Long Legs.
Too sad mourning the unknown diseased.

Oh, let's just call a spade a spade.
There is no logical reason for no rhyme.
It could be excessive flights of fantasy
or simply being too lazy.

26

Gratitude

When next you see me in a season,
after geese have flown south,
after trees have huddled together from
       north winds,
I shall have survived.

When sunset fades over grassland prairies
and subsequent darkness brings no pain,
when sunrise means a hopeful feeling
that anything is possible, blessed healing,
I shall have survived.

I am factually grateful for my genetics,
as how else could I appreciate well-being
and all that I have gained?
I am aware of kindness in a profound way,
priceless bounty straight from the heart—
how shall I repay that which has no cost?

During these now-easier moments,
I preview difficulties to come—
ashes of my youth lying inside an urn,
an outcome I do not fear but do not yearn for.
I am emotionally better prepared for life,
better educated as if granted a diploma
on gratitude.

27

I'm Nobody

(inspired by Emily Dickinson)

I'm nobody. Who are you?
I'm a nobody who hides in plain sight
as chameleons do.

Who walks through a room and no one will stare
because to them I'm not even there.

Who can eat at a table with no flash in my face,
publicizing my meal all over the place.

Who stands in a line, looks up to the sky,
and marvels how birds can rise up and fly,
while Somebody Else, Someone known
        and pursued,
has to lower her head and keep her eyes glued
to the sidewalk, the crosswalk, the aisle in
        the store,
literally keeping her eyes on the crumbs on
        the floor.

While Me, a Miss No One, can slide down a slide,
take a walk in the rain with a friend by my side,
glide into a bake shop with cakes near the door,
saying, "Let me eat cake,"
without headlines exposing the tight clothes
        that I wore
or the size of my ring or my hair—what a bore!

What a joy to live like a private last class,
a recluse, a relic, a thing from the past,
who is free without asking to wander in town
and to do as she pleases, her feet on the ground,
with the wind at her back, her spine straight
        and tall,
a little Miss Nobody, not Someone at all.

28

Winter's Coming

Bees are buzzing
this time of the year.

Not a second to spare, not a minute to watch
         the news,
there is work to be done—
a single-minded purpose
in the gardens by the mews.

Darting in the noonday sun,
supple marguerite daisies bending
from a breeze by the bay, genuflecting.

Bee wings beating furiously, as if to say,
"Time's wasting, leaves are turning to rust,
winter is on her way, red berries ripening,
but no time for a break when you are a busy bee.
Winter's coming, no use longing for a
          warmer clime,
for an onshore voyage to a field of dreams."

Working all the time, working 'round the clock,
fragile bee wings propelling hither and yon,
kneeling, reeling, swiftly lifting
tired bee eyes up to the heavens above,
above all the sluggards on earth.

29

Devotions

Monks in a monastery,
heads bowed, eyes closed, lips reciting:
"Make me an instrument of Thy peace:
where there is hate, I may show love,
where there is offense, I may show pardon,
where there is discord, I may show harmony,
where there is error, I may show truth,
where there is doubt, I may show faith,
where there is despair, I may show hope."

I believe a smile is stronger than a weapon.
I believe in the power of a generous hand.
I believe anger is a weakness, not a show of force.

Direct me toward love and compassion,
not to be consoled but to console,
not to be understood but to understand.

For it is in giving that I receive,
for it is in selflessness that I find myself,
for it is in dying that I will be resurrected.

Made in the USA
Middletown, DE
11 December 2023

45223842R00040